To Mary Lou!

Best wishes!

Ron Maslin
11/4/15

What I Believe

God is not Exclusive

By Ron Madison

Cover art from a painting by Johnson,
from the collection of the author who
purchased it from the artist in 1969.

Printed in the U. S. A

First printing: 2015

ISBN 13: 978-1-887206-28-0

Ron Madison on You-Tube:
"It's a Beautiful Story," Dr. Ron Madison@TEDx Johnstown
"Ned and the World's Religions," by AIB

To my son David,
who inspired me to let go,
enjoy life and write.

Content

Introduction

I am not an expert on religions, and this is not a reference-work. This is simply an introduction—an exposure to the beauty that lies within the great religions. It is an opportunity for better understanding. My purpose is to expose you to the fact that there is beauty and kindness in these religions and in the people who believe in them, and there is much we can learn from them.

We have become a world in which we are bombarded by ideas…through the media, our friends, our politicians, our families. Ideas come at us so fast, couched as truths, that it is difficult for us to take the time to be skeptical of them. We have become far too gullible—if enough people believe, it must be fact.

From my previous work, I found to my surprise that I had much to learn from children, who see the world from an entirely different view than I do. Their perspective is a simple and innocent view not yet influenced by prejudice—not yet concerned about the future.

I recently found that I had much to learn from teenagers as well. Teenagers see the world from another view. Theirs is a view overloaded with conflicting information. They have become skeptical of almost everything, searching for their own identity, terribly concerned about what the future holds for them. It's not so much they disbelieve what they have been taught, rather they are simply trying to figure out how all of this relates to the world around them and to their own lives. It is a wonder today's teenagers cope, but indeed they do.

It would be easy to dismiss teenage thinking as being that of immature minds, not really worth taking the trouble to listen to. But that would be wrong. To cope in today's world and to face the future without putting our head in the sand, we need to have the flexibility, the acceptance, the problem-solving skills and the skepticism of a teenager.

There are certain things which teenagers wrestle with in the privacy of their own thoughts, things they are rather shy about submitting to open debate, things that are not really "cool" to talk about. Religion is one such topic, and that is what I'd like to discuss, because it is an important part of those things that teenagers are trying to sort out. It is a subject that most of us need to better understand, to help us cope in a world that is getting smaller and more complicated.

As you read, my own thoughts will be obvious, but for the most part, I am not the author…I am the typewriter.

Thoughts from Teenagers

Thoughts from Teenagers

An effort to learn more about the world's religions at the college level in the United States has been going on for over twenty years. That effort has been getting stronger as college students realize the importance of understanding the world's diverse cultures if they are to be successful in a modern world. That need is just now beginning to be recognized by high school students.

I thought I would pass on to teenagers what I had learned while doing the research for my previous book, *Ned and the World's Religions, as seen through the eyes of children*. But first, I had to find out if such an approach would even work.

I talked to my friends at the Greater Johnstown School District, who had worked with me in the past when I had sought input from elementary school children on two other books: *Ned Learns to Say No, a lesson about drugs*, written at the request of the Superintendent of Schools; and *Ned and the General, a lesson about deployment*, written for the U.S. Army.

What I offered to give them was a comprehensive exercise in taking an idea, in this case an idea for a book, and learning how to flesh it out in a way that would result in a final product that would be meaningful to the targeted audience—how to develop an idea into a sellable product. What I hoped to get in return was far more complicated—to learn how to think like a teenager!

The Principal supported the idea and arranged for me to work with a group of gifted high-school students. The class consisted of eight students, including freshmen, sophomores and seniors.

When I first met with the students at the beginning of the school year, I was quite nervous. I was delving into what was for me a new genre, and I was working with a more mature group of kids than I had in the past... really smart kids.

I explained to the students that when I write a children's book, I have to pretend I am a child. That's easy for me to do because I once was a child, and the child that I once was would be very much at home in today's world. Writing a book for teenagers would be much more difficult for me, because even though I once was a teenager, the teenager I once was would be lost in today's world. I needed their help in learning how to communicate with today's teenagers.

After laying down the challenge, I left them with a drafted copy of the book to review for our next meeting.

When we met the following week, they were brutal—they challenged my ideas and took exception to my approach. After the original shock, I realized they were being critical, but supportive, which was exactly what I had wanted.

I looked forward to these sessions throughout the school year, and with each session, what I wrote became better.

The final session near the end of the school year started at the beginning of their school day and was scheduled to continue as long as the discussion was fruitful. We were still going strong at the end of the day when Rob Heinrich, their teacher, hit them with a pop quiz. He gave them just ten minutes prior to boarding their buses for home to answer what he called "Reflection questions." The questions were:

"Why should people (teens in particular) read this book?"

"What did this book do for you personally?"

I was puzzled. Why did he wait until the last minute to ask the questions? How did he expect them to intelligently answer such thought-provoking questions with so short notice.

But I was glad he asked. I was eager to know how many of the students had found the subject (as opposed to the exercise) to be of personal interest to them. I'd hoped one or two might. I was wrong…they all did, and their responses are worth sharing:

"Why should people read this book?"

"People should read this book because it challenges us to think outside the box. It provides the basis for many new ideas and outlooks on life. Teens are at a time in life where we're trying to find our identities, and this book provides wholesome ideas to help us do that."

Angelique Stolar-Hall, 12th Grade

"Adolescence is the stage of confusion and insecurity. Teenagers are constantly looking for guidance and assistance, and this book shows how seemingly contrasting religions, or no religion at all, can serve to open one's mind to new ideas—religion, academic or otherwise."

Jonathan Skufca, 12th Grade

"It opens your eyes to how similar the religions of the world are. It truly shows that all religions connect, and being bound by only one keeps you from seeing all the beauty of the world."

Kayla Leventry, 9th Grade

"I feel as though this book will help someone who is having trouble with/in their search of new beliefs and ideas. It covers a wide range of topics in an insightful and informative way, but allows any readers to draw their own conclusions."

Benjamin Herdman, 9th Grade

"This book provides insight not only to the variety in the world but also to the variety in our lives and how we can learn from one another."

John Smith, 12th Grade

"It really makes you have a time period for opening your mind and being able to, in that time, break down all the complexities of religions, allowing for the idea that is wrapped underneath the sacred texts to sink in and take effect."

Andrew Constable, 12th Grade

"Teens should read this book because it gives them an insight on the different beliefs around the world. Instead of just knowing and preaching the religion of their parents, it allows them to open their minds about the many other religions around the world."

Jessica Salem, 12th Grade

"The time for open-minded spirituality has truly come. As more and more teens reach the critical point in their development, where blind acceptance turns into questions, this book will act as a sort of bridge into healthy acceptance of world religion and a life led in moral wisdom."

Joseph Pannone, 10th Grade

"What did this book do for you personally?"

"This book opened my eyes to the many different beliefs and religions around me to find my own truths in what I believe."

Angelique Stolar-Hall, 12th Grade

"As someone who has a rather strong Catholic faith, this book allowed me not only to appreciate the beliefs of others but also to recognize the similar drive we all have—to lead fulfilling lives."

Jonathan Skufca, 12th Grade

"This book opened my eyes to how connected most religions really are. No matter what we believe, we all have the same basic belief and that is that we should be nice to each other."

Benjamin Herdman, 9th Grade

"Personally this book opened my eyes; it took an idea I was not interested in and conveyed it in a way which made me rethink what I do in my own life."

John Smith, 12th Grade

"It helped me to further understand the lives and beliefs that have been followed for hundreds of years. Also furthering the questions I often wonder about myself."

Andrew Constable, 12th Grade

"This book helped me better understand different religions. It showed me that it isn't necessarily all about just believing and preaching your religion, it is about accepting and appreciating the beliefs of others."

Jessica Salem, 12th Grade

"This book truly opened my mind in a spiritual sense and resolved the almost negative feelings that come with questioning a religious mindset formed by a fundamentalist household."

Joseph Pannone, 10th Grade

How I Learned to Admire the Faith of Others

How I Learned to Admire the Faith of Others

In the summer of 2006, Dr. Gerald L. Zahorchak, then secretary of education for the state of Pennsylvania, asked me to write a children's book about the world's religions, a book that he could use in the schools. It sounded like a great idea, so I thought I'd give it a try.

And so I began what I hoped would be every bit as eye-opening an experience for me as the previous book I had written, *Ned and the General, a lesson about deployment*, which I wrote for the U. S. Army as an aid to help children cope with the trauma of a parent's deployment. When I started that book, I had no concept of the complexity of the problem or just how much I would learn from the children who were in the process of trying to live with their fear and anger.

As a result, I wasn't unprepared for the surprises in store for me on this new journey, but I had absolutely no idea what a profound effect it would have on my own life and beliefs.

Let me tell you about it.

There are nearly two billion Christians in the world, over a billion Muslims, nearly a billion Hindus, and half a billion Buddhists[1]. It was obvious to me that

---

[1] The world's total population is seven billion.

those four great religions should be included in the book. It is not at all clear from the data which religion might be in fifth place, but that was not important. I felt it was important to include Judaism, the precursor of the world's two largest religions. Judaism, along with Christianity and Islam, considers Abraham to be the first of the great prophets. I also wanted to include Native Americans, because of my own curiosity and because I thought the children might be intrigued.

That's how I came to focus on six religions: Christianity; Islam; Hinduism; Buddhism; Judaism; and Native American.

I certainly wasn't an expert on the world's religions, and I quickly realized I never could be. But I knew children, and I believed that if I could find the right children, they would tell me what I needed to know. It wouldn't be so much a book on religion; it would be a book on how children *feel* about their religion. If I could only find the right children, I could bring their stories together in a book of easily flowing rhyme that children might enjoy. It would be a book based on children talking about what *they* believe. *They* would be the guides, and it would be *their* words that would inspire, not mine.

But how do I find the children, children who are smart enough and devout enough to be able to tell me what it is they believe? Could I possibly expect to find such wisdom in a ten-year-old child? I had no idea, but I did know the only way I could accomplish the task was to begin the search. It wasn't that I found the children or that they found me, but it did happen. Somehow, it all came together.

Lindsey, a Methodist Christian

The first child I interviewed was Lindsey. She caught my ear during a gathering of young children at a Methodist church in a suburb northeast of Atlanta, GA. The Pastor was talking about love. The children spoke out, trying to outdo each other, trying to impress their favorite pastor. That's when I heard Lindsey, who was sitting next to me, say as if she were thinking out loud: "I don't tell my mother I love her anymore when she comes to kiss me goodnight; I tell her I Christ her."

The next day I had an opportunity to ask Lindsey what she meant by her unusual comment the previous day. She replied, "We use the word love in so many ways today, it doesn't mean much anymore. But when you think of how Christ loves us, that's special."

My hunch was right—I could find these children, and Lindsey was to be my first.

Gazal, a Hindu

The second child I interviewed was one of Lindsey's friends from her Brownie troop: Gazal, who is Hindu. Needless to say, I was apprehensive. I knew very little about the Hindu faith and had never had a friend who was from India. I was afraid I might inadvertently do something to offend them. But Gazal and her family quickly put me at ease.

Gazal's father explained to me that Hinduism is a very inclusive faith that embraces many religions and has many forms. "Even a Christian could practice his religion within the Hindu faith," he said. I am still struggling with that thought but have come to the realization that it is not important that I believe it; what is important is that he believes it.

I asked Gazal, "If you could tell children all over the world what it is you like about being Hindu, what would you tell them?"

She talked about Yoga, which she does every morning as a prayer. She talked about her favorite holiday, the festival of Holi. And she talked about her favorite manifestation of God, Ganesh.

I explained to Gazal's parents, "In order for me to write Gazal's story, I have to pretend I am a Hindu child. I can easily pretend I am a child, but I cannot pretend I am Hindu. Will you help me?" They trusted me, invited me into their lives and enabled me to pretend I was Hindu.

The time I spent with Gazal and her family was a revelation for me. The Hindu traditions, rituals and methodology were quite different from my own. Yet, I found the same underlying message of love and the same respect for humanity and all life. The time I spent with them praying in their temple, was a time spent in a holy place—a time, if you will, spent not so much with their God or my God but with our God.

Yet I had trouble understanding how Hindus could believe in a single God when my visits to their Temples revealed many altars for many Gods. I was told that it is the Hindu concept that Brahman cannot be thought or spoken...Brahman is beyond comprehension. All the things they call God are simply images of the incomprehensible.

In that respect, I guess it's no different from the many saints of Catholicism or the eagle of the Plains Indians. How does one pray to an entity one cannot even comprehend? For many, it is far easier and far more personal to seek an intermediary—a manifestation of that God based on myth or legend or story or utility, as in Hinduism; a holy person or a saint, as in Catholicism;

or the animal that can soar the highest and therefore be closest to God, the eagle, as in the culture of the Plains Indians. We do a similar thing in our everyday life—when we want to approach someone whom we feel is unapproachable, we seek an intermediary, someone we trust, someone whom we feel can carry the message for us.

The approach I used with Gazal and her family worked so well in helping me understand Hinduism that I used it as a model for the other children I would interview for the book.

Max, a Jew

Max is from Naples, FL.

I have always felt certain warmth when I am with my Jewish friends, and Max, smart, witty, always smiling, made me feel as though we had been friends for a long time. I went beyond the bounds of politeness and teased him by asking him what we Christians beg to ask our Jewish friends, but never dare to: "Do you really believe the Jews are God's chosen people?" Most religious people you pose that question to would say, "Yes, of course." That's why they feel so strongly about their religion; they honestly believe God chose them.

After thinking about the question for a moment, Max

said, "That's what we're taught." He paused for a moment, smiled and said, "I believe God chose us to give the Torah." Then he added, "And I believe God chose us to give the Ten Commandments."

In his wise and modest way, he confirmed, at least in one sense, that the Jews were God's chosen people.

I had the honor of attending a Yom Kippur service as the guest of a dear friend. Yom Kippur is the Jewish Day of Atonement. I joined the congregation in prayerfully trying to recall those I may have wronged in the previous year and making an honest vow to seek them out and atone for those wrongs. The thought occurred to me, as a Christian, that Yom Kippur is part of my roots. The better I understand Judaism, the better I will understand Christianity.

Ricky, a Native American

I met Ricky, an Arapaho, on the Wind River Reservation in Wyoming.

In the Arapaho culture, it is the role of the grandparents to educate the children, the role of the aunts and uncles to discipline the children and the role of the parents to love the children.

Ricky's grandmother on his mother's side was a Shaman. She raised him to be an Arapaho warrior—

taught him the religion, the language, the dance, the culture. Ricky's grandmother on his father's side was Catholic. She raised him in the traditions of the Jesuit missionaries she loved so dearly. Ricky is, in fact, a devout Roman Catholic Arapaho warrior!

I was amazed that Ricky was able to combine the two cultures without sensing any contradiction. And yet, the more time I spent with Ricky and his people, the more I realized there is no contradiction between their ancient beliefs and their Christianity.

There are many people throughout the world who, like the Arapaho, have taken the best of two or more cultures and crafted for themselves a life-ethic that works well. When you stop to think about it, it would be difficult today to find a religion that has not evolved from a combination of beliefs or a religion that has not been tampered in some manner by the needs of the times.

Ricky asked me one day to join him with a few of his extended family for an afternoon of prayer at their sweat lodge. I was honored and excited, because I knew Ricky considered the sweat lodge to be his favorite form of prayer. As we drove to the lodge, Ricky explained to me that I might find the experience quite uncomfortable. "By suffering as we pray, our prayers are more likely to be heard," he said. The lodge was about twenty feet in diameter and looked like a large turtle shell from the outside. The frame was covered with skins and blankets in such a manner as to ensure that no light entered the enclosure. There was a roaring fire nearby, heating several large rocks to be used in the ceremony. We entered the lodge through an open flap, which was also the only source of light. Following the lead of the others, I sat on the ground at the perimeter and faced the center.

Once we were seated, several large rocks, heated from the fire, were placed in a pit that had been dug in the center of the enclosure. The entrance flap was then closed, and we were plunged into complete darkness. Water was poured on the rocks, filling the lodge with hot steam. Then the prayers began—each person alone with his thoughts and his God. Someone began a slow, steady beat on a sacred drum. After about ten minutes, I was quite cramped, hot and sweaty and had trouble breathing. I bent backwards, lying flat, so I could fill my lungs with cooler air. Ricky had suggested I do that if I felt faint. A short time later the flap was opened, and we all filed out. We breathed the dry prairie air for five minutes while the rocks in the pit were replaced with fresh ones from the fire. I handled the second session a bit better, though I still felt uncomfortable. It was during the third session that I was able to settle in, relax and as Ricky would say:

"As I prayed and sweat,
every care and sin
seemed to ooze from my body,
and peace came in."

I passed on the fourth and last session; I was exhausted. I had experienced what I came for—to share with my Arapaho friend his favorite form of prayer.

While on the reservation, I had an opportunity to meet with an elderly Shoshone who knew of my interest in working with the Shoshone and Arapaho children on the reservation. He spent an afternoon with me explaining many things about the Native American culture that he thought I should know. I learned much from this learned man, and if I may pass on to you only one of his thoughts, it would be this: "When you ask me a question," he said, "I will not answer you immediately, for in our culture such an act would be considered an insult. It would mean I did not respect you enough to give serious thought to your question before I answered."

Karma, a Buddhist

I met Karma at a Buddhist Monastery in Woodstock, NY, during a Fire Puja, which is part of the weeklong preparations prior to Losar, the Tibetan New Year. A Puja is a prayer rite celebrated around a fire. I was given a few sprigs of evergreen. I watched Karma and, following his lead, circled the fire and threw the sprigs into the flames. As I watched them burn, I could feel at peace as I imagined my troubles being consumed in the sacred fire. The purpose of the rite was to begin the New Year the following day with a clean heart. For Buddhists, it is a prayer for the expulsion of the bad karma in all people, not just themselves. It is a prayer for the world.

I remember sitting earlier that day in the Shrine of the monastery listening to the monks pray. They sat in Yoga fashion, with legs crossed, and in a very low pitch chanted the prayers blessing the coming New Year. Each prayer ended with the sounding of a gong, the tinkling of hand bells and the low moan of ancient mountain horns. I felt in a sacred place and privileged to be joining in a solemn and ancient prayer.

I knew that Karma's grandparents had made the arduous trek from Tibet over the Himalayas to Nepal, then to India, before settling in the U. S. I wanted that story, and I wanted it told in Karma's words. But as soon as his mother realized where I was headed, she gently excused herself, and she and Karma left me... alone and embarrassed. Later that day over lunch at the Monastery, I told those with me at the table what had happened and that I felt I had unwittingly done something to make the mother feel uncomfortable. An elderly Tibetan gentleman sitting across from me simply said, "He does not know."

The man went on to say, "It is the Buddhist tradition that one does not dwell on events or people who have caused us pain. For to do so does nothing to change the pain of the event or the wrong that has been done to us. The only result is to make us, ourselves, angry as we relive the pain. The child does not know what happened. He has not been told."

What Karma wanted to talk about was the Dalai Lama, who had visited Woodstock two years prior. Karma told me a beautiful story the Dalai Lama had told the children, and it is this story that became "Karma's Story" in the book.

A few years later, when I was at The Parliament of the World's Religions in Melbourne, Australia, I had the opportunity to show the Dalai Lama the story. He liked it and autographed the page in the book where it appeared.

The Dalai Lama, a world-renowned Buddhist leader, was the spiritual leader of Buddhist Tibet before it was annexed by China. Because the Chinese government was trying to control all religion at that time, it became necessary for the Dalai Lama, when only twelve years old, to leave Tibet and make the difficult and dangerous journey over the Himalayan Mountains to Nepal and then to India.

I met a young Buddhist monk who had made a similar journey. Tashi Gawa, an artist, was painting the elaborate ornamentation of the new Buddhist Monastery in Woodstock. He was born in 1971 in a mountain village in central Tibet near Lhasa, the capital. He told me that when he was a very young boy, the magnificent old monastery in the village had not been used for many years and was in great disrepair. The monks had long ago been scattered and were gone. His early education was in a government school, where ethics and philosophy were taught from a little red book written by China's Communist Leader Mao Tse-Tung.

Over time, things changed. The villagers began to rebuild the old monastery, and some of the monks returned. Tashi Gawa found himself going to the monastery after school to hear the monks talk. It was out of curiosity, as he knew nothing about Buddhism, which had been forbidden by the government for years, and he believed, as he had been taught at school, that Buddhism was nothing but the foolish nonsense of old men. He went to the monastery because it was something to do after school…and it was a bit daring. There he met an old monk, who made a great impact on the young Tashi Gawa. What that wise man had to say about the teachings of Buddha made the teachings of Chairman Mao seem insignificant by comparison. As a thirteen-year-old boy, Tashi Gawa entered the monastery and became a Buddhist Monk.

Karam, a Muslim

There is a small mosque in Windber, PA, near where I live. I got to know the Imam, who introduced me to young Karam and his family. They are a wonderful family, but I felt intimidated by Karam's father… needlessly so. I knew that if I had any hopes of gaining support from the family in my quest to better understand Islam, it was the father, the patriarch, I would have to win over.

For whatever reason, I found myself uncomfortable writing Karam's story. I was searching for perfection, and what I was able to write was far from perfection. When the time came to share the story with the family, I felt embarrassed. As I sat and watched the family read the poem I had written based on what Karam had told me, my eyes were glued to his father's face, searching for a clue as to what he was thinking. I found myself slipping further and further down into the overstuffed chair that trapped me, trying to hide as I imagined his stern visage change from concern to scowl. Finally, without changing his expression, he looked at me over the top of his reading glasses and said quietly, "It's beautiful."

Karam's family, all Muslim, have been American citizens for many years, and the three children were born here. They live nearby, in Somerset, PA, so I have gotten to know them well. They love America as much, or more, as their native Palestine and feel at home here. But their lives changed significantly after 9/11. In the eyes of friends and neighbors and fellow workers, they found themselves being associated with that horrendous act. Time, fortunately, has healed much of that ill will.

Lillian, a Baptist Christian

I thought it would be helpful to touch upon the wide diversity that exists within religions. That's why I interviewed Lillian. I wanted a story that would contrast with Lindsey, a quiet Methodist from Atlanta, GA and was led to Lillian, an outgoing Baptist from West Chester, PA.

Lillian told me she liked going to church on Sunday— it was fun. Thinking back to when I was her age and what I then thought about going to church, I could hardly believe a young child would consider going to church "fun." But when I joined her for a two-hour service the following Sunday, I had to admit she was right—the choir was outstanding, the singing of the congregation—robust, the dancing—spiritual, the readings—inspirational, and the sermon—like fire and brimstone. It was the first time I'd ever been in a Baptist church but certainly not the last. It *was* fun, and I learned having fun can be a beautiful and powerful form of prayer.

Lillian started dancing when she was four years old. Two years later, following her older sister's lead, she joined the Dance Ministry at her church and loved it. She had found a special way to pray, using the talent she felt God had given her.

I was not familiar with Dance Ministry. Even with Lillian's attempts to explain it, I did not understand what was different or special about this type of dance. Then I saw her dance, and I knew. I realized how dancing can be a beautiful form of prayer.

I had felt the same thing when I had watched the dancers of tribes from all over the Northwest at the Shoshone Sun Dance. They too were Christian, and they too were performing a prayer dance—a dance handed down to them from their ancestors.

I have attended religious services in many Christian denominations and have found much that is the same. Over many years, each group has developed a way to pay homage to Christ in a manner they feel is the most respectful, and so it should be. The same is true of the various divisions among other major religions.

Ned, the protagonist

When Ned, the main character in *Ned and the World's Religions, as seen through the eyes of children*, heard his friends' stories, he was amazed…and hopeful. What he realized was this:

> *Even though we disagree*
>> *Our lives can create great harmony.*
>> *Each in our own and separate way,*
>> *Each together as one voice say:*
>> *Love of God, and all it might mean;*
>> *Love of neighbor, though hard it may seem.*
>
> *Truth, respect and charity too:*
>> *These are the things we all should do.*
>> *And of all these things, one stands above:*

> **To honestly, truly learn to love.**

Getting past the Differences

There you have it: Lindsey, a Methodist Christian girl, and Gazal, a Hindu girl, both from Atlanta, GA; Max, a Jewish boy from Naples, FL; Ricky, an Arapaho from the Wind River Reservation in Wyoming; Karma, a Buddhist boy from Woodstock, NY; Karam, a Muslim from Windber, PA; and Lillian, a Baptist girl from West Chester, PA.

With each of these children and with their respective families, I was able to immerse myself into their lives and beliefs to the extent that I could truly pretend I was the young child whose story I was retelling.

Do you have any idea what a profound effect that had on me?

Once I reached the point where I could pretend to be a certain child, I found I could truly understand and have empathy for what that child believed. It completely changed my view of the world, the people who live in it and what they believe. The beauty was that I could see all these beliefs from the perspective of an innocent child who I had grown to know and to respect and to love.

I found I was able to get past the differences and discover the common theme that seems to be a part of all of their beliefs. We call it The Golden Rule:

> *Do unto others,*
> *as you would have them do unto you.*

Beautiful Stories

Beautiful Stories

The passion that the families I interviewed had for their respective religions encouraged me to study their sacred texts, so I might better understand their motivation. I found them to be beautiful stories—each written for different people in different places at different times, for people who lived in different circumstances and had different needs, for people whose understanding was often limited and who sometimes needed to be motivated by fear and controlled by strict rules.

Sometimes we fail to grasp the beauty of these stories because we don't think they are true. Maybe that's a misconception on our part.

Perhaps there is truth in fiction. We know that if we want to learn the "truth" of the physical world, we can turn to science; and if we want to learn the "truth" about history, we can turn to archaeology. But if we want to learn the "truth" of the human reaction to events, of how humans responded, interpreted and explained the events that took place in their lives, and in doing so shaped our lives, then we must look for answers in the writings of the times—mythology, lore and sacred texts.

In reading these sacred texts, I had to be careful not to interpret them solely based on my own limited exposure and experience. It would be better, I felt, to leave any such interpretations to religious scholars who dedicate their lives to helping us understand what these texts meant to the people for whom they were initially written.

I had to remind myself not to condemn these stories just because I don't understand them or because they are sometimes interpreted in ways that foster personal gain in wrongful and sometimes evil purposes.

I found these stories have much in common…so much so, that I believe they may have had the same Author. Or perhaps the human mind was somehow destined to produce such a result. Or did such stories evolve from nothing over the millennia, just as the mind itself has evolved?

I've found these stories can stir the mind, move the heart and lead one to a better life. No one person can read them all, but if each one of us could read just one and accept its beauty and honestly try to live by it, and if we could at the same time listen with an open mind to the beauty in the stories that others read and honestly try to live by, then how much better we would be able to understand others, understand the world in which we live and understand ourselves.

And the world just might be a better place for us all.

Spirituality

Spirituality

There seems to be an inner drive in all of us that makes us different from the animals. It is more than a drive for sex and food and survival. It manifests itself in each of us in different ways.

How we respond to that drive is what makes us who we are.

As a result of that drive, we find ourselves seeking something in our lives that is meaningful: fame; compassion; artistry; accomplishment; love; the good life; or maybe just comfort.

Writers and philosophers have talked of this drive for centuries as though it were an enigma no one has really quite figured out. Recently, they have coined a term for it: SPIRITUALITY. In its modern use, spirituality is not necessarily considered to be a religious term.

I recently read a description of spirituality from Ron Rolheiser's book, *The Holy Longing*[2]. I found it very appropriate to what we have been discussing and would like to include a few of his thoughts for your consideration:

"It is no easy task to walk this earth and find

[2] The Holy Longing. The Search for a Christian Spirituality, Doubleday, 07/99

peace. Inside of us, it would seem, something is at odds with the very rhythm of things, and we are forever restless, dissatisfied, frustrated and aching. We are so overcharged with desire that it is hard to come to simple rest...

"What we do with that [desire], how we channel it, is our spirituality. Thus, we all have a spirituality whether we want one or not, whether we are religious or not. Spirituality is more about whether or not we can sleep at night than about whether we go to church. It is about being integrated or falling apart, about being within community or being lonely, about being in harmony with Mother Earth or being alienated from her. Irrespective of whether or not we let ourselves be consciously shaped by any explicit religious ideas, we act in ways that leave us either healthy or unhealthy, loving or bitter. What shapes our actions is our spirituality.

"We can see from all of this that spirituality is about what we do with our spirits, our souls... [Spirituality] has to give us energy and fire, so that we do not lose our vitality, and all sense of beauty and joy of living. Thus, the opposite of a spiritual person is not a person who rejects the idea of God...the opposite of being spiritual is to have no energy, to have lost all zest for living...

"Our soul is not something that we have; it is more something that we are. It is the very life-pulse within us, that which makes us alive. Thus, we speak of someone as dying precisely when the soul leaves the body. That is accurate. The soul is the life principle within a human person, as indeed it is the life-pulse within anything that is living. As such, it has two functions:

First of all, [our soul] is the principal of energy... It is full of energy, eros and all the things that eros carries—desire, disquiet, nostalgia, lust, appetite and hope. Eros is soul, and soul gives us energy.

[Second of all, our soul is] the adhesive that holds us together, the principal of integration and individualization within us.

The soul not only makes us alive, it makes us one."

Why Religion

Why Religion?

Spirituality has been a driving factor in human development over the centuries, leading to a search as to who we are and why we are here. Ever since the dawn of civilization, humankind has believed in some kind of being or force beyond them. Why is that so? Was it simply a way for people to help explain the unexplainable?

How did such beliefs evolve to become what today we call "religion?"

At what stage in the development of human society did this belief become a way to help foster and enforce a sense of the greater good of the group over that of the individual?

Was religion simply the result of evolution, of natural selection? Or was it, as these people apparently believed, something beyond the natural world?

Are you aware that religions have offered more than just a philosophy of life? Over the centuries:

> Religions have offered an opportunity for membership into a community—an opportunity to join with others, especially those with shared challenges and interests.

Religions have offered the aspect of ritual to life. Many of these rituals have led to extraordinary works of art: painting, sculpture and music. In some cases, the rituals themselves are considered works of art.

Religions have acknowledged the passage of time with seasonal observations, annual festivals and activities and formal acknowledgment of special passages in life such as birth, marriage and death.

Religions have been one of the best chroniclers of history; and even today, they have a profound effect in shaping history.

Religions have provided the foundations for law and order within and between societies.

Have you ever wondered why there are so many religions in the world? Have you ever thought that perhaps it is supposed to be that way, so that each individual can enjoy the wonders of God in a way that suits that individual best? Perhaps it is so humankind can share with each other the best of what has been learned and believed over the centuries, so that the best thoughts might prevail.

Christianity, Islam, Hinduism, Buddhism, Judaism and Native American

Christianity, Islam, Hinduism, Buddhim Judaism and Native American

For those of you who know little about these six religions, let me provide you with a brief background.

Christianity

Christianity was founded as a Jewish sect by followers of the prophet, Jesus, whom Christians believe is the son of God. Jesus was crucified in 30 CE[3] . Christians became distinct from Jews after the Romans destroyed Jerusalem and its Jewish temple in 70 CE.

The sacred texts of Christianity were written between 75 and 150 CE and were later compiled into a single text called the Gospels in 335 CE. In the year 325 CE, the Roman Emperor Constantine became a Christian; and in 380 CE, Christianity became the official religion of the Roman Empire.

> *"In everything, do unto others*
> *as you would have them do unto you."*
> *Jesus, Matthew 7:12*

---

[3] CE refers to the year of the "Common Era." Christians use the notation AD (Anno Domini), referring to the year after the birth of Christ.

Islam

Islam traces its roots to Abraham, as does Judaism and Christianity. Islam was founded around 650 CE by the Arab prophet Mohammad, who built upon the foundations of Judaism and Christianity and who considered Jews and Christians to be brothers in faith. The teachings of Mohammad were compiled in the Koran, the sacred text of Islam, shortly after his death.

> *"Not one of you is a believer until you wish for others that which you wish for yourself."*
> *Number 13 of Imam, Al-Narawi's Forty Hadiths*

Hinduism

As old as the Abrahamic religions are, Hinduism predates them by several centuries. Hinduism consists of a great many diverse traditions and, because of that, has no single founder. It traces its roots to the ancient Vedic religion and is considered to be the oldest religion in the world. Scholars estimate that the Vedas, the sacred scriptures of Hindus, were compiled prior to 4,000 BCE [3].

> *"This is the sum of duty: do not do to others what would cause pain if done to you."*
> *Mahabharata, 5:1517*

---

[3]BCE refers to the year before the "Common Era." Christians use the notation BC, referring to the year before the birth of Christ.

Buddhism

Buddhism was founded around 500 BCE by Siddhartha Gautama, the son of a Hindu royal. His followers called him The Buddha (The Enlightened One) and spread his teachings throughout the Eastern world.

Although Buddhism is recognized as a religion, many people consider Buddha's teachings to be more philosophical than religious. That is why many Christians and Jews, as well as Hindus, follow some of Buddha's teachings as a part of their own faith. Much of the Buddhist philosophy is grounded in meditation and yoga, both of which are ancient Hindu practices, which The Buddha encouraged.

> *"True affection leads to tolerance,*
> *forgiveness, happiness."*
> *The Dalai Lama, Woodstock, NY,*
> *September 26, 2006*

Judaism

Judaism traces its roots to the prophet Abraham, about 2,000 BCE and at a later date to the prophet Moses, who gave the Jewish people The Ten Commandments, the foundation of Jewish law. Moses also passed on to them many revelations, which became the basis for their holy book, The Torah.

"What is hateful to you, do not to your fellowman. This is the entire law. The rest is commentary."
Talmud, Shabbat 3id

Native American

Not much is known about the origins of the Native American religions. The religion of the Plains Indians that I encountered, the Shoshone and Arapaho, was apparently quite similar to that of Christianity and many of them were converted by Episcopalian and Jesuit missionaries in the 1800s.

"All things are our relatives; what we do to everything, we do to ourselves. All is really one."
Black Elk

Atheism

Atheism

I want to digress for a moment from what I learned writing *Ned and the World's Religions* and talk about a subject that was raised a short time ago during my first session with the students at the high school. It was Angie Stolar who asked,

"Why don't you talk about Atheism?"

She asked it critically, more as a challenge than a question. I had not yet developed a rapport with the students, and the electric atmosphere that ensued made me realize that if I answered the question poorly, I would exacerbate the distrust I felt the students already had toward me. These sessions, which were so important to me, would come to a quick end.

I knew the students expected a thoughtful response to what I thought was a stupid question. I tried very hard to come up with a compelling answer, but the best I could do was respond with what I thought was a very logical reply,

"Because Atheism is not a religion."

As soon as I said it, I knew it was not the answer the students wanted to hear.

Angie shot back, "It is a perfectly acceptable way of

life, and that is what you are talking about in your book, isn't it?"

I found myself on the losing end of the debate, and I decided to pursue Atheism, not because I thought they were right, but because they felt it was necessary, and they represented my target audience.

Throughout these sessions, the students were critical of what I had written (or failed to write), but they made a sincere effort to be helpful. Regarding Atheism, they encouraged me to meet with Wes McMichael, a professor of philosophy and world religions at the local junior college. Several of them were taking college accredited courses there, and he was one of their favorite professors.

So I invited Wes to join me for coffee one morning before class. It was the first of several delightful meetings, and the two of us became good friends. Wes, a self-declared Atheist, had once been a Baptist minister. Before meeting Wes, I assumed that all Atheists were anti-religious, but much to my surprise, I found Wes by no means anti-religious. I would even go so far as to say Wes McMichael is pro-religious...but he does not believe in God. Like me, he is convinced that each of us needs to believe in something, and he encourages his students to do so.

Thanks to Wes, I've replaced my preconceived notions about Atheism with a much better understanding and appreciation.

Just what does it mean to be atheist?

"Atheism" is a word derived from the Greek "a," meaning "without," and "theos," meaning "God." So a literal definition of an "atheist" would be "one who is without God." Sounds simple enough, but actually it gets quite complicated, and there are more than one version of being "without God."

According to Wes, an Atheist may be a nihilist, an adherent of a world religion, or a secular humanist.

A Nihilist

"A Nihilist," he said, "believes that there is no value in existence." The term comes from the Latin "nihil," which means "nothing." Nihilism is a rejection of all religious and moral principles in the belief that life is meaningless.

An Adherent of a World Religion

Wes advised me that someone could be an adherent of a world religion and yet not believe in a God in the same sense that others do. Buddhists, for example, do not believe in a creator God, and many of them would consider themselves Atheists.

A Secular Humanist

Wes tells me that the worldview most commonly held by Atheists (and by him) is "secular humanism." Wes believes he must find meaning and purpose in a short, single life, and he believes that relationships and virtue are valuable in and of themselves. It is a philosophy that looks for natural explanations for every occurrence— there are no supernatural entities (or, at least, none that affect anything in the universe in any way), and there is nothing after life. Science and philosophy serve as the only tools for understanding and interpreting the world.

None-the-less, Wes appreciates the fact that many (and probably most) of the world's greatest scientists and philosophers have been religious and have sought to gain a better understanding of the nature and beauty of the works of God through the tools of science and philosophy.

A secular humanist, such as Wes, shares a most important pursuit with religious people—a pursuit to find a morality that will serve humankind and help identify an ethical framework by which to live our lives.

As Wes pointed out to me, "There is beauty in the worldview of secular humanists just as there is in the world's religions. I think this beauty can and should be celebrated as well."

I happen to be a Christian, and I believe in the same moral ethic that my Atheist friend does. The only difference between my thinking and his is that he chooses to do it without the need for God. He bases his moral ethic on human reason. I, personally, feel I need more help than that.

George Farley, whom I met several years ago in Melbourne, Australia, advised me that I should include Atheism in any discussion of the world's religions. George is a close friend of the Dalai Lama and founder of the Australian Tibetan Association. It was George Farley who arranged for the Dalai Lama to sign my book. I consider George to be a very religious man, so I was surprised he would feel so strongly about including Atheism. I have since learned much more about Buddhism and can better understand why George feels this way.

The more I learned about Atheism, the more I realized that Angie Stolar, the Greater Johnstown High School student, and George Farley, the Australian businessman, were right—I should include Atheism in this book. As a matter of fact, the largest interfaith group in the world, The Parliament of the World's Religions, includes Atheists within its membership.

The Parliament of the World's Religions

The Parliament of the World's Religions attempts to bring harmony and understanding among the world's religions. This group first met at the Chicago World's Fair in 1893, when religious leaders from all over the world came together in answer to an invitation from a visionary and well respected Hindu, who lived in Chicago.

The Parliament of the World's Religions last met in Melbourne, Australia, in December of 2009, with nearly 8,000 dignitaries from most of the world's religions along with others interested in promoting interfaith dialog. It is undoubtedly the most inclusive and universal of the many groups worldwide that attempt to find mutual understanding among the world's religions.

The top four religions were well represented, as were virtually all of the recognized religions of the world, and there are far more than I would have thought. Each religion and group had an opportunity to showcase who they are and what they believe. But more important than the opportunity to showcase was the opportunity for these diverse groups to engage in dialog about their commonality, about how they could learn from each other and about how, through mutual understanding, they could help the world become a better place.

I was invited to attend The Parliament in Melbourne as a "Guest Author" because of my book, *Ned and the World's Religions, as seen through the eyes of children*. I attended along with my son Mike and my dear friend, the Reverend Dr. William E. Carpenter, a Methodist Minister and my mentor in writing the book.

With help from Bill and Mike, I led a workshop titled "Teaching Children about the World's Religions." Much to our surprise and pleasure, it turned out to be a standing-room-only event with attendees from a wide range of religions, including Hindus, Buddhist, Jews, Christians of many types, Jains and Sikhs. We found the group supportive of our efforts and quite interested in the idea of exposing young children to the ideas of religious harmony.

The three of us came away from The Parliament pleased with the knowledge that so many people throughout the world are trying to break down the barriers and to promote harmony among the world's religions. It was a tremendous reinforcement to what I had learned while writing the book.

When you think of the great commonality of the major

religions, why is it so hard for us to find it? Why must we seem to labor so intently on our differences? How much simpler could humanity's relationships be if we would truly attempt to understand people who see things differently from us and learn to get along and be able to accept them, not as Christians, Jews, Muslims, Hindus, Buddhists or Native Americans, but as neighbors and, perhaps, friends.

On the flight home from Melbourne, Bill, Mike and I began to discuss plans for a workshop at the next Parliament. Our workshop at Melbourne had been a standing-room-only success, the two hundred copies of *Ned and the World's Religions* we took with us were eagerly sought and many of the people we met encouraged us to continue the effort at the next Parliament. We had touched a nerve—teaching children about the world's religions had become a hot topic.

Shortly after returning home, I emailed the executive director and asked that he consider a series of workshops on the topic for the next Parliament. I realized we'd need lots of help if we were to get such a topic included in the agenda, so I copied two of the most influential people I had met in Melbourne: George Farley, founder of the Australian Tibetan Association, and D. R. Kaarthikian, former Secretary General of India's Human Rights Foundation.

It turns out that "youth" will be one of the major topics of the 2015 Parliament of the World's Religions, to be held in Salt Lake City, Utah, in October. I will be presenting a workshop along with Audrey Galex, the producer of a video of *Ned and the World's Religions, as seen through the eyes of children*. The Video was produced and televised by Atlanta Interfaith Broadcasting, Atlanta, GA. The workshop is titled "Teaching Children about the World's Religions" and will be based on the video and this book, *What I Believe*.

What I Believe

What I Believe

If you have stayed with me this long, I think I owe it to you to tell you what I believe. My goal is not to convince you to believe as I do…you need to make your own decision as to how to live your life. I simply ask you to hear what I have learned in the hope that you may find it of use.

I was born and raised a Roman Catholic Christian. I still am. But after what I have learned these past few years, I have a much more profound love of my faith than I ever had.

There is an understandable fear that if we are to be truly open to the beauty of other faiths, we must surely lose our own religious convictions.

Don't believe that for one moment!

The Power of Skepticism

I happen to be a trained scientist. When I received my Ph.D. from Lehigh University, I knew as much about my narrow field of expertise as anyone in the world—which is the nature of Ph.D. studies. As I look back on those years, I am amazed how important faith is in the scientific community. I'm not talking about religious faith; I'm talking about faith in those who have worked so hard in our field before us. But in the scientific world, that faith is always couched in a sense of skepticism:

Is it really true?
How can we understand it better?

I have found that a strong dose of honest skepticism of my religious faith, just as happened in my scientific faith, has been a healthy and rewarding experience. I love the Catholic Mass; I love receiving communion even though I know that what we do is not at all like how the first Christians celebrated…nor is it supposed to be. It is simply a beautiful event crafted and honed by Christians over the centuries as an expression of love.

The Power of Ritual

Ritual is an important part of my Catholic faith; and although I have been exposed to it all my life, it was just a few years ago that I began to understand the powerful sense of community that ritual can provide.

It happened on an Indian reservation in western Wyoming. I had been invited by the Shoshone Indians to be a guest at their annual Sun Dance. I rode with them in the back of a pick-up truck to the river, an hour's ride away, to gather cottonwood logs and branches to build the ceremonial lodge. That night, I watched them bless the ground on which the lodge would be built. The next day, I helped them build the lodge for the performance of the dance...one side left open to allow an unobstructed view by the community. The ceremony lasted continuously for four days.

When I attended the first morning's session of the Sun Dance, I hadn't a clue what was going on. I found myself a bystander, watching others perform what they believed was a powerful prayer to the same God I believed in. I tried as best I could and said a few of the prayers I learned as a child, but it didn't work. I felt awkward, strange and out-of-place. I was convinced that everyone there thought I was awkward, strange and out-of-place.

And then I remembered what my Shoshone mentor had told me about the ceremony I attended when the Shaman blessed the ground on which we built the Lodge. The ceremony was highlighted by the sprinkling of cedar shavings accompanied by the leader's chant and the rhythmic beating of the tribal drum. "What were they chanting," I asked my mentor, "what were the words?" He replied, "Our chants have no words; they have meaning...and everyone knows the meaning."

So I forgot about trying to find words. I tried instead to get a sense of the meaning of what they, the performers and the community, felt...and it worked. I couldn't always understand the prayer, but I found I could be a part of it. Sometimes the meaning was obvious, like when the young lad in his Army uniform ready to ship out to Afghanistan stood before the dancers and the Medicine Man and when the young girl with an obvious cancer stood before them.

It suddenly dawned on me: it's not the ritual that is important but the meaning; it's the fact that everyone knows the meaning; and it's the fact that all the participants can share that meaning as a community. That's the beauty of it. That's the beauty of ritual.

The Beauty of Sacred Texts

All the major religions of the world have their sacred texts. I do not read the scripture of my own faith as a way to justify what I believe; I read it to gain insight in how I might better live my life. What is more, I can read the sacred texts of other faiths not only to better understand what those faiths believe but also to learn what those faiths can teach me in trying to lead a better life. I search for the beauty in those texts.

What is Beauty?

In one of the many sessions I had with the students from the Greater Johnstown High School, I raised the issue of beauty. I began the discussion by introducing the following thought:

> It seems we try too hard searching for beauty and wonder why we don't find it. Perhaps it is the baggage we carry that hinders us, thinking we know what it is we are looking for—searching for the familiar, the comfortable, the pleasant. Better to simply let go, open our eyes and our ears, our minds and our hearts, and simply let beauty find us.

Much to my surprise, that thought led these students to a discussion of one of the most pervasive subjects of their own inner-debate—how they look! I could not help but think of my own teenage years and the impact "looks" had on me and on my peers. It was bad back then but apparently nowhere near as bad as it is today.

I listened to their release of frustration for a long time, adding a word or two when I thought it might help…it didn't. Obviously they had reason for concern.

We are constantly bombarded by visions of beautiful people selling us things, telling us things, willing us things. So much so that those visions, and the people we see in them, have become the standard, the norm. Anything less has become less—less normal, less real, less desired. In spite of the fact that only a very few highly paid people actually meet those standards, we subconsciously let those visions become the standard of the "Body Beautiful" for those around us and for us, ourselves. No wonder so many people are unhappy; we have set an unattainable goal of how people should look.

Until we can willfully cast aside what has brainwashed us, until we can honestly look at ourselves in a mirror and see BEAUTY, the beauty God has created in us, the beauty of who we are and what we are, how can we ever hope to find beauty in our lives?

A Personal God?

Although the scientist within me cautions against it, I do believe in a personal God. Why? Because it works for me. It brings me great comfort to think I am not alone—to think there is someone out there who cares for me and the good or bad I do.

I believe God loves us all and wants us all to share in that love. I believe the greatest show of love was given by Jesus Christ twenty centuries ago at his crucifixion. I believe all of us can learn from that great act of love, whether we are Christian and consider Him the Son of God, Muslim and readily accept him as a great prophet, Jewish and can accept such an act of love from one whom we do not believe was the messiah, or any of the hundreds of other faiths who know of him: the Jesus of history.

Having said that, I ask you to accept the fact that it is not my role here to argue for or against religion or to advance any particular religious belief. That is for you to decide for yourself.

What is Truth?

There was a time when I thought I knew TRUTH. I no longer believe I do, and I no longer get hung up on the need to find TRUTH. Although I constantly search for knowledge, I actually hope I will never find the TRUTH. For it is the searching that enriches my life, and it is my faith that helps me be a better person. If, God forbid, I should ever think that somehow I had found TRUTH, I would have no need for faith or to search.

Perhaps my fear is that if I ever found TRUTH, life might lose its beauty. What's worse, if I found TRUTH, I might not like it—it might not be at all what I have always loved, found beautiful, felt inspiring. What if TRUTH, for example, is utter nothingness? Although some might embrace it, to me that would be a horrible thought. I have learned to enjoy my life, to enjoy the constant search for knowledge and to enjoy the beauty around me.

I have found there is great beauty and purpose brought into my life through religion, a religion that provides me with beliefs that help me lead a better life and a religion whose traditions and pageantry I find beautiful and which strengthen my belief.

I have learned to enjoy my faith far more now than when I started this journey. And I have learned to find beauty and inspiration in what others believe.

What do You Believe?

What do You Believe?

I've tried to be honest with you in sharing my thoughts about what I have learned in these last few years.

Children, I found, have quite a different perspective on life than we do—more innocent and open, full of hope and without prejudice.

I have learned from the children. Perhaps that is why I have been so open in telling you what I believe. In return, let me ask you:

"What do you believe?"

If you have not yet asked yourself that question, ask it now. Ask it with the innocence of a child—openly, full of hope and without prejudice. But ask it with all the respect and thought and love that are due to the most important person in your life—you.

What is it that drives you in life, makes you feel like it is all worth the while? What is your SPIRITUALITY, as Ron Rolheiser would ask?

If you believe in God, be aware there are many paths to him. Choose the one that best suits you, but choose one. If you are fortunate enough to have a strong faith, don't worry about losing it by being skeptical…you won't. Faith is a gift to be treasured.

If you do not believe in God, know there are many paths that will help you lead a responsible and fulfilled life; choose the one that best suits you. But choose one.

If you want to bring sense and beauty and direction into your life, believe…

Believe in something.

Acknowledgements

Acknowledgements

My heartfelt thanks go out to the many people who have helped me in this effort. I'd like to mention a few to whom I am most indebted:

my son David, who gave his life in the service of his country and in doing so caused me to relook at my own life. As a child, his favorite book was *Ferdinand the Bull*;

my wife and children and grandchildren who edited, inspired and encouraged my writing;

my editor, Sarah Pastorek, who did so much to make my stilted writing flow and gave me encouragement when I most needed it;

my artist David Covolo, who created my character, Ned, and illustrated and laid out all my books;

my mentor, the Reverend Bill Carpenter, who helped me negotiate the intricacies of the religions I studied;

my long-time friend and fan, Jerry Zahorchak, who sent me out on a journey to learn about the world's religions;

my pastor, Father Mark Begly, for his encouragement;

my test lab, the Greater Johnstown High School, particularly Rob Heinrich and his students;

and the children and their families who helped me learn to appreciate the beauty of their beliefs.

About the Author

Other Books by Ron Madison:

Ned's Head,
a lesson in self esteem

Ned and Fred,
a lesson in loyalty

Ned, Fred and Friend,
a lesson in compassion

Ned's Friend,
a lesson in friendship

Ned and Crow,
a lesson in diversity

Ned's Folks,
a lesson about love

Ned's Hat,
a lesson about safety

Ned and the Gift of Life,
a lesson about blood
(written for The American Red Cross)

Ned Learns to say No,
a lesson about drugs

Ned and the General,
a lesson about deployment
(written for The U.S. Army)

Ned and the World's Religions,
as seen through the eyes of children

About the Author

For me, these years were a time of reflection. My children were grown and had children of their own. I had finished the career I had worked so hard to prepare for, and I had retired. It was time to buy that home in Florida, relax and enjoy my grandchildren growing to adulthood.

But I didn't. Instead, I set out on a new career. I focused on the fun I had found creating stories for my children and then my children's children. What began as fun-filled rhymes actually became lessons for children—lessons in self-esteem, loyalty, friendship, compassion, diversity and love. That led to books addressing social issues such as safety, drugs and the deployment of military mothers and fathers…all told from the perspective of children. And then to the life-changing journey and research for the writing of my last two books.

Prior to becoming an author, I was a teacher and researcher, leading to management positions in the steel and then the utility industries.

My formal education resulted in a master's degree from The University of Washington and a doctorate of philosophy from Lehigh University.

I was raised in Shaker Heights, Ohio, lived as a newlywed in Hermosa Beach, CA, began my family in Oakland, CA, and raised my children in Bethlehem, PA, and Flossmoor, IL. My wife and I now live in Johnstown, PA.